Make My Day!

More Cartoons by Pat Oliphant
Foreword by Bill Mauldin

Andrews, McMeel & Parker
A Universal Press Syndicate Company
Kansas City • New York

Foreword

In the twenty-one years since he immigrated here from Australia, Pat Oliphant has established himself as the most successful American political cartoonist of this century. Some five hundred newspapers buy his work, some one hundred colleagues slavishly imitate him, and his penguin trademark has become a national institution.

He deserves all this. He has an abundance of all the qualities one needs in his profession: artistic talent, intense skepticism, devastating humor . . . and most important of all, total iconoclasm.

It is probably this last quality which answers a couple of paradoxical questions about the career of my young friend Patrick. (He's pushing fifty but I speak from the pinnacle of somewhat more advanced age.)

First, why has he not been employed by a major newspaper since the *Washington Star* sank under him? The truth is that every publisher who can afford him is scared of him. We are slipping back into an era of journalistic dullness comparable to that of the thirties and forties. If you hire a firebrand such as Pat you are more or less obliged to print all of his work. It is much easier (and cheaper) to buy his syndicated services and use those cartoons that don't shake you up. (Mind you, Oliphant doesn't burn down a barn *every* day. Sometimes he just waves lighted matches about in a teasing manner.)

Second, why has Oliphant but one Pulitzer Prize instead of half a dozen, while far lesser talents boast two and three? The answer to that one is a standing rebuke to the people who dish out the prizes. Back in 1967 Pat decided an important award would help his career in his new country, so he made a careful study of cartoons which had previously won Pulitzers. He accurately deduced that they seemed to fit a pattern. He hoked up a drawing of Ho Chi Minh carrying a dead child in his arms.

"They won't get us to the peace table, will they?" chortles the old Red.

Dead children always grab Pulitzer judges, as do anticommunist themes. Pat slipped this turkey in with ten or so of his more legitimate entries and of course it won. Now, Oliphant was not the first cartoonist to pull this stunt, nor will he be the last. But he made the mistake of telling a few friends about it. At least it was a mistake if he was greedy for more Pulitzers, which I doubt. I said he was an iconoclast, didn't I?

He is a major contributor to national sanity. Long may he wave.

BILL MAULDIN

'COMRADE SAKHAROV MERELY HAS THE SNIFFLES.'

'STOP, IN THE NAME OF THE LAW!'

DR. FINKELSTEIN WAS LAST SEEN BEING DRAGGED FROM HIS CAR TO A WAITING GOVERNMENT VAN. AUTHORITIES SAY THAT HE IS PROBABLY BEING FORCED TO TREAT MEDICARE PATIENTS FOR A FIXED FEE. THE CAR WAS NOT DAMAGED.

June 25, 1984

'BECAUSE HE OWES ME A DOWN-PAYMENT ON DA INTEREST HE OWES ME ON DA MONEY HE BORROWED, OR I'LL BREAK HIS KNEES, SEE? — DAT'S WHY DA BUM NEEDS A LOAN!'

'A MR. JACKSON HERE TO FREE SAKHAROV!'

July 3, 1984

12

'GEORGE, I MAY HAVE TO SEND YOU OUT FOR A SEX-CHANGE OPERATION.'

'WHO AM I, DOCTOR? I MEAN, WHO AM I, DOCTOR? I MEAN, WHO AM I, DOCTOR? LIKE, I MEAN, WHO AM I, Y'KNOW? WHO AM I? TELL ME, WHO? WHO? WHO?'

'ALMOST PERFECT — SHE'S FEMALE, SHE'S BLACK, SHE'S JEWISH AND SHE SPEAKS SPANISH...
SHE ALSO SAYS TO STAY OFF HER DADBLASTED PORCH.'

'SCRAP IT AND ORDER A NEW ONE — THE ASHTRAYS ARE FULL.'

July 13, 1984

'AT LAST, GERALDINE, I'M DOING SOMETHING I'LL BE REMEMBERED FOR.'

18

'RIGHT THERE IS WHAT WE CONSERVATIVES NEED! — WHERE CAN WE GET A JESSE JACKSON?'

July 16, 1984

'HOW SIMPLY DIVINE! THE FERRARO LOOK WAS JUST **MADE** FOR MR. BUSH.'

July 19, 1984

OFF IN SEARCH OF WINDMILLS.

July 20, 1984

23

'GENTLEMEN — TO OUR LEAN, MEAN FIGHTING MACHINE!'

'I NEVER COULD UNDERSTAND WHAT THEY'RE SAYING IN THESE TRACK ANNOUNCEMENTS.'

'STEP UP AHEAD OF ME, WALLY — WE WOULDN'T WANT ANYONE TO CONFUSE OUR RELATIVE POSITIONS.'

August 6, 1984

TEN YEARS ON

'HOW 'BOUT A LITTLE DRINK TO RE-REGULATION...'

"LEFT AT THE HEAD OF THE STAIRS, PAST THE GAYS-FOR-TROTSKY MEETING, THE LESBIAN-CHRISTIAN-ALLIANCE COUNCIL, THE BAPTIST BIBLE MEETING, AND THE COVEN MEETING IS ON THE RIGHT, CAN'T MISS IT!"

SLEEP WELL, CAPTAIN —THE PASSENGERS AND CREW ARE ALERT.

AN AGENT OF THE DELOREAN STING OPERATION TACKLES HIS NEW ASSIGNMENT.

August 27, 1984

ALL THOSE TEACHERS OPPOSED TO SCHOOL PRAYER PLEASE MOVE FORWARD TO THE LAUNCH AREA...

'YOU SLAM UP THE WINDOW AND STICK YOUR HEAD OUT AND YELL,"I'M MAD AS HELL, AND I'M NOT GOING TO TAKE IT ANY MORE!!" NOW, CAN WE HAVE IT WITH FEELING..?'

'HI. MY NAME IS WALTER AND I'M YOUR BLIND DATE.'

'ATTENTION. THE LUGGAGE PREVIOUSLY PROMISED FROM EARLIER SCREWED-UP FLIGHTS IS NOW ARRIVING AT THE BAGGAGE CLAIM AREA. MAYBE... SORT OF. THANK YOU.'

48

September 25, 1984

HOSTAGES

1980...1984

THIS YEAR WAS GETTING TOO DULL, ANYWAY.

MR. DONOVAN IS TAKEN BY THE DREADED SLEAZE.

AFTER SHUDDERING TO A HALT FROM A TEMPORARY LACK OF FUNDS, THE MIGHTY MACHINERY OF THE UNITED STATES GOVERNMENT SLOWLY GRINDS BACK INTO MOTION.

October 8, 1984

October 9, 1984

'SOME PEOPLE TO SEE YOU, MR. PRESIDENT — YOUR DRAMA COACH, YOUR SPEECH COACH, YOUR DEBATING COACH, YOUR IMAGE TECHNICIAN, YOUR KITCHEN REMODELER, ER.. ETCETERA.'

OLD MAN REAGAN'S FLY BALL

October 15, 1984

'HERE'S YOUR ALLOWANCE INCREASE, SON...ER, MAY WE EXPECT YOU TO START EARNING YOUR KEEP, SOON..?'

GREAT ISSUES OF 1984

'READY?'   'READY!'

'SOME OF THESE GUYS MUST HAVE BETRAYED ME!'

'HEY, RONNIE, WHAT IF THERE REALLY ARE GHOSTS WHICH I KNOW THERE AIN'T BUT WHAT IF THERE REALLY IS, RONNIE NOT THAT I'M SCARED OF COURSE BUT WHAT IF...?'

October 29, 1984

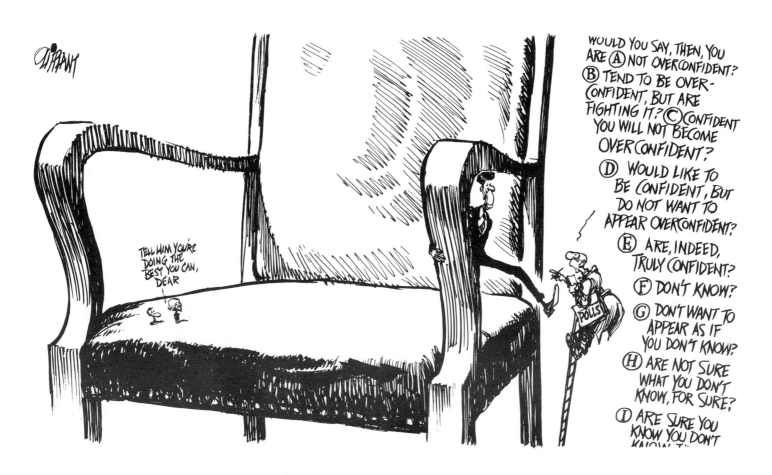

November 1, 1984

'...AND WHOSE LITTLE DOGGIE ARE YOU?'

THE COAT-TAILER.

'YES, SIR—RAISE TAXES, AND BEGIN BOMBING IN FIVE MINUTES. WILL THERE BE ANYTHING ELSE..?'

'THAT'S JUST A HARMLESS LITTLE TAX REFORM SNAKE, HE'S NOT GONNA HURT YOU — C'MON, GET GOING.'

AMERICA'S FIGHTING BISHOPS REDISTRIBUTE THE NATION'S WEALTH.

November 20, 1984

November 21, 1984

December 4, 1984

AFRICA'S BURDEN

".. NOW, TO CATCH THIS SIMPLIFIED TAX SNAKE, JUST GRAB IT BY THE TAIL WITH ONE HAND AND VERY QUICKLY RUN YOUR OTHER HAND ALONG IT, UP TO ITS HEAD — SIMPLE!"

December 6, 1984

December 12, 1984

"EXCUSE ME...AM I ON THE RIGHT BUS FOR LEADERSHIP?"

A GREAT TIME OF YEAR TO ANNOUNCE A POSTAL INCREASE.

'YOU'RE STARVING BECAUSE OF CAPITALIST NEGLIGENCE, THAT'S WHY—NOW, SHUT UP AND EAT YOUR BOOK!''

"NOT ONLY DID THEY OFFER ME A BLOOD LIBEL — THEY ALSO HURT MY FEELINGS!"

December 28, 1984

'THE WHITE HOUSE IS CALLING FOR 200 CLEAN-CUT, ALL-AMERICAN TYPES TO PLAY THE INAUGURAL — HEY, RAMIREZ, GARCIA, LÓPEZ, GONZALES, RODRIGUEZ...'

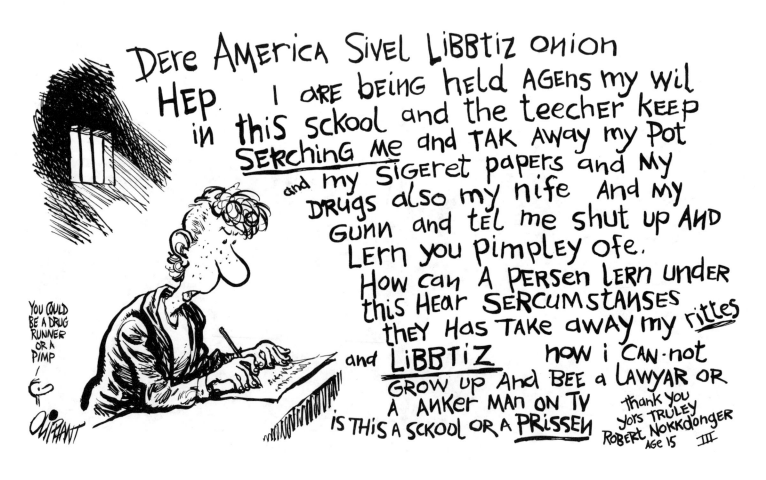

January 18, 1985

'ANN LANDERS SAYS HERE THAT MOST WOMEN WOULD RATHER SETTLE FOR A CUDDLE, THAN COMPLETE THE ACT —WADDA YA SAY TO THAT, ANIMAL??'

'WE WAS LISTENIN' TO AMERICA SING, WHEN SUDDENLY BERTIE FROZE UP.'

'OH, HENRY, I DO HOPE THE TALL, THIN YOUNG MAN IS OUR MUGGER — HE'S JUST <u>SO</u> CHARISMATIC!'

January 24, 1985

'COME ON, JEANNIE — OPEN THE DOOR, NOW. UNCLE RONNIE HAS A LOLLYPOP FOR YOU, AND GUESS WHAT!!
IT'S A GREAT, BIG INTERNATIONAL DEVELOPMENT LOLLYPOP! M·M·M·M·YUM! JEANE, OPEN THE DOOR!'

January 25, 1985

ONE OF THE NOT-UNFIT-TO-SERVE CROWD

THE VERDICT

'THERE, NOW—I'M ALL SET TO BECOME PRIME MINISTER.'

113

January 29, 1985

THE SMOOTH TRANSFERENCE OF POWER, SOVIET STYLE.

114

February 1, 1985

117

'PICK IT UP, MAGGOTS — THIS HERE'S THE NEW REVOLUTION YOU'RE IN!'

February 12, 1985

'YOUNG MAN, I HOPE THAT EXTRA TWO CENTS WILL ENSURE THE SWIFTER COMPLETION OF YOUR APPOINTED ROUND.'

February 22, 1985

SAINT JOAN — A REMAKE

126

FARMERS FIRST

HELP. I AM BEING HELD IN A RAT-INFESTED MEXICAN PRISON.

'CAPITAL CITIES COMMUNICATIONS, DO YOU TAKE THIS... ARE YOU SURE YOU WANT TO DO THIS?'

March 20, 1985

March 22, 1985

NO LIMIT ON PAC MONEY

MAKING ANIMALS OF US, INDEED!

THE SUPREME COURT REVERSES EVOLUTION

March 26, 1985

THE SOVIETS HAVE EXPRESSED REGRET FOR THE MURDER OF A U.S. ARMY MAJOR IN EAST GERMANY... AND NOW, ON TO GENEVA.

TRADE WARS

'WELL, LESSEE... IRON BALL, LARGE, PROB'LY RUN AROUND 10 GRAND APIECE, 2 FEET OF CHAIN, HEAVY, AT $3,500 A FOOT, ONE IRON BRACELET... HOW MANY OF THESE UNITS YOU NEED?'

'IT'S WAR, MA — WE'RE GONNA HAVE TO CRASH THE JAPANESE EASTER EGG MARKET!'

April 4, 1985

'OK, IT'S OFFICIAL, FOLKS! JEANIE KIRKPATRICK HAS JOINED THE REPUBLICAN PARTY—LET'S HAVE A BIG HAND FOR THE LITTLE LADY, FOLKS! C'MON, LET'S HEAR IT FOR JEANE, A GREAT GAL! YEAAA.'

'...AND LOOK SINCERE!'

April 8, 1985

April 10, 1985

HEY, JAPAN—BUY AMERICAN!

'... HOWEVER, AS AN OPPONENT ONE MUST ADMIT HE IS A MOST ENGAGING PERSONALITY, AND A CHARMING AND WITTY CONVERSATIONALIST. I AM GONNA MOIDA DA BUM, ANYWAY!'

April 18, 1985

'THIS IS THE RIGHT-WING CBS EVENING NEWS, JESSE HELMS REPORTING. BIASED NEWS-CASTER, DAN RATHER WAS BURNED AS A COMMIE WITCH TODAY. IN OTHER GOOD NEWS...'

SOON AFTER PLANNING THE PRESIDENT'S GERMAN VISIT, ADVANCE-MAN MICHAEL DEAVER LEFT THE WHITE HOUSE FOR A POSITION WITH THE PRESTIGIOUS PR FIRM OF FEINSTEIN, COHEN AND WEINBERG.

April 25, 1985

THE ART OF RECOGNITION

'SORRY — THESE ARE STUDY AND ADMINISTRATIVE FUNDS.'

'THAT'S NOT ALL — THE BULL GOT LOOSE!'

'WE APPRECIATE THE HUNDRED MILLION DOLLAR OFFER, BUT TELL MR. MURDOCH WE AIN'T SELLIN''

May 8, 1985

May 10, 1985

162

'FIRST THE WHEEL, NOW THIS — THINGS ARE GETTING OUT OF HAND!'

May 16, 1985

'WE ASKED CITY HALL TO GET "MOVE" OUT OF OUR NEIGHBORHOOD, AND YOU MUST ADMIT THEY
HAVE BEEN VERY RESPONSIVE TO OUR COMPLAINTS.'

May 20, 1985

'JEEZ, USE SOME DISCRETION, WILL YA? MY PROCUREMENT PRACTICES ARE UNDER REVIEW!'

May 22, 1985

May 23, 1985

'A THOUSAND PARDONS, BUT PERHAPS IT WOULD BE HELPFUL TO MOVE THE FINISH LINE DOWN TO THEM.'

May 29, 1985

174

WHAT WILL THE SIMPLIFIED SYSTEM MEAN TO YOU? : PART 1.